Call of the Sidhe

Magical Poems by
WB Yeats and GW Russell (AE)

Call of the Sidhe

Magical Poems by
WB Yeats and GW Russell (AE)

Art by Jeremy Berg
Commentary by Søren Hauge

Lorian Press LLC

Call of the Sidhe

Magical Poems by
WB Yeats and GW Russell (AE)

Art on page 46 by Deva Berg
All other art by Jeremy Berg
Cover design by Asha Hossain
Edited by Susan Sherman

Published by Lorian Press LLC
Douglas, Michigan

ISBN: 978-1-939790-36-1

Hauge, Søren
Call of the Sidhe/Søren Hauge

First Edition August, 2021

www.lorian.org
www.lorianpress.com
www.wildheart.land

Dedication

*To the Guardians of the
Gateways of Peace*

Table Of Contents

Preface

It is not every day one can enjoy the privilege of honoring some of the great poets of the world, and at the same time highlight some of the most treasured themes of one's life. This is the case with the book you are reading right now. I have the tremendous joy of offering highly needed attention to two notable souls and their outstanding contributions to the reality of the Sidhe. My hope is to create an awareness of the deeply relevant partnership we can make with our close relatives as we start unfolding our own inner and almost forgotten Sidhe-nature. In partnership, we can contribute to the healing of our highly tested global home, the very Earth we inhabit.

I want to give special thanks to Sussie Luscinia Nielsen for her unique participation in reflecting on the deeper significance of the poems of W.B. Yeats and George William Russell, known and referred to here as AE. As a core part of the process, Sussie created melodies to songs of the poems, and it is hoped that these songs will one day be available for listeners around the world. Until then, it is possible for everyone to listen to her singing *"The Song of Wandering Aengus"* by Yeats from her award winning third album, *"Pigens Morgen"*, that was released in 2006 and received the Danish Music Award in 2007 for best album in the Folk genre.

I am especially grateful for Jeremy Berg's invitation to the making of this special book and for his ability to catch the Sidhe inspiration when it blows in the wind. Not only is Jeremy a gifted artist and publisher, but he is a trusted friend and a genuine pioneer in the field of Sidhe-human collaboration with his own unique approach as a teacher and facilitator that began with the emergence of the Sidhe Card Deck and has unfolded since.

Also special thanks to my friends Marian Angel Costa, Aaron Samuel Jean Crombe, Ben van Haeff and Michael Jones who have leaned into the newness of Sidhe-fellowship with me with a spirit of artistic adventure, and to Hanne Vibe Andreasen for vital and deep inspiration into the field of gentle-wild leadership and the emerging Sidhe-awareness.

If any reader is new to this theme, I warmly recommend David Spangler's excellent books, *"Conversations with the Sidhe"* (2014) and *"Engaging with the Sidhe"* (2017) as they give perspective and a wealth of details. Having said that, I will add that David's deep insights and personal perceptions constitute the best research I can think of, and his natural, careful, and humble approach to this and other spiritual topics is so rare and profound that I owe exceptional gratitude to him for what he does and is. I also give him my deepest thanks for supporting what I share in relation to the Sidhe.

The Tradition

If we were to talk about 'the missing link' in Human history, the Sidhe would be the true candidates for this role. Sidhe (pronounced *Shee*) is a Gaelic word meaning *The People of the Mounds,* but the name has many meanings and connotations that open doors to our understanding of the Sidhe, our closest relatives. In the Celtic tradition they are known by many names including *the Gentry, the People of Peace, the Good Neighbors, the Good People, the Gentle People* or simply *the People*, but they are also called *the Faery people, the Faeries* or *the Fey.* They should not be confused with the Little People, a term referring to nature spirits like gnomes, flower fairies, mannikins, undines, goblins, dryads, etc.

In the Nordic countries they are known as *the Elves*, but more frequently as the *Huldra People,* meaning the hidden people, which is a clue to their relationship and position to humanity. They are a people and remarkably like us in many ways, yet also quite different. Communication with them has revealed a story of a common past. Once we were one family, one life-stream evolving like the main trunk of a tree. Later when divisions arose which resulted in different ways of living and evolving, humans and Sidhe became more akin to separate branches of this family tree. We humans have distanced ourselves from the Sidhe, making them into mythological creatures, figures in science fiction, ancient superstition, and figments of our imagination. The Sidhe are neither immortal semi-Gods or flower fairies – the latter being a species of nature spirits in the deva kingdom – but are our equals and in a way are also our ancestors as we share a common origin. They truly are our closest relatives, and we can cooperate with them in service for Gaia or the Earth and the larger wholeness we are part of. Today we witness a gradual renaissance in the knowledge of them, but it is not just a novelty as insights about them go far back into the distant past.

A Greater Reality

Many of us humans tend to assume – in our slightly narrow-minded reality – that the world exists for us and that we are supposed to rule the planet. We have grown accustomed to the belief that we are the superior species here on Earth and that other living beings are at our disposal and convenience as pets, resources or even products. In our materialistic and technological arrogance, we have taken decisions about what we think is real and what is significant – and then projected it on our surroundings without asking any other beings. As we define life according to narrow physical and biological criteria we believe the only reality is physical and everything important revolves around our needs. To a large degree we do whatever we fancy and most often it is measured from financial and purely material interests.

However, this picture does not hold any longer. In fact, it is extremely outdated, even according to natural science. The cracks in the physical wall have become huge crevices. Materialism turns out to have been a tiny interplay on a long journey. Death is not the end of our evolution. All living beings have soul as everything originates from the divine source. The physical world is only the densest floor in the huge mansion of the house of life. Other dimensions are knocking on the door. The cosmos is teeming with life inhabited with countless beings and we need to let go of previous prejudices and make room for a reality that surprises, amazes and astounds us. The reality of angels, nature spirits and elemental beings are some of the rediscoveries in the multidimensional reality. In this vast realm we need to make room for yet another category of co-beings. They have always been here, but we have reduced them to being products of an imagination gone wild.

Not The Usual Fairies

In recent times, the word "fairy" has been associated with

small, magical flower-creatures, nature spirits connected to the plant kingdom and the beauty of nature. Such creatures do exist, and they have been romanticized and interpreted in cute ways that partly reflect human needs and reality. Shakespeare's (1564-1616) *"A Midsummer Night's Dream"* shows us that an abundance of nature spirits was part of public consciousness. Fairies were part of local faith in many forms. They were the Little People about three feet tall and less, all the way down to insect size. However, sometimes they were also portrayed as giants. The term fairy covered a range of creatures. Edmund Spenser's (1552-1599) huge book *"The Fairy Queen"* (1596) is an example. Alexander Pope (1688-1744) revived the idea of tiny and delicate flower fairies. In the Victorian period nature spirits – fairies – were imagined as often being insect size and this remained the most popularized perception into our time. These poets and many others from the Renaissance and forward caught impressions that are partly real, partly constructed, but all relating to nature spirits that belong to the deva or angelic kingdom.

The 'traditional' fairies are not just human fantasies, but they are neither connected to the Irish Faeries that open the door to what here is called the Sidhe. Confusing as it may be for new readers, the Irish Faeries are perceived as human and humanoid size or greater, and they are a people, not creatures relating to flowers, water, wind, earth, and other elements. Many people confuse traditional fairies with the Sidhe, and it is not difficult to understand why as the Sidhe have a deeper connectedness to nature than we humans.

The Underworld

The Sidhe tradition is alive around the world, and in western civilization there is precious wisdom to be found in areas like Ireland, Scotland, and Iceland, plus several other regions. However, the Irish-Celtic tradition is especially rich with knowledge and awareness of the Sidhe woven into the very core of history and culture. Unless you have been exposed to certain groups and teachers who are deeply into teachings of the underworld and certain angles of nature wisdom, it is highly likely you have never heard about the Sidhe before. Until recently much concerning the Sidhe has been under the radar. Perhaps, at least symbolically, it coincides with the fact that the Sidhe themselves have been called *the Hidden People*, and the most prevalent Nordic name for them is *Huldra People* which means disguised or veiled people.

Mainstream spirituality has not been focused on the underworld but has been about higher consciousness and reaching up, not down. That does not mean that the Sidhe are only related to below, but tradition often calls them the inhabitants of the underworld. The reason for this focus is partly because of the lore regarding their discreet or 'under-the-radar-existence', living beneath sacred mounds and stone circles. This is not the whole story, but the symbolism holds because the Sidhe are behind the veil of our solid physicality. They are incarnated themselves, but in a more subtle manner. Another word for the abode of the Sidhe that might be much more fitting, is perhaps the Otherworld. However, the truth is that there is only one coherent reality consisting of many realms, and we humans belong to that very same totality or wholeness. We are simply inhabiting different, overlapping frequencies of it.

If we stay with the word underworld, I suggest we use the following analogy. Let us consider 'under' to be beneath the surface. In that way 'under' means in the deep or simply depth. Compare that to how we humans experience existence. We experience the world as a surface. We are surface people. That is also how we tend to perceive the world in the so-called modern or post-modern era we are part of right now. We are living our lives on the surface of the planet, and we seem to be very skilled in outer measuring and manifesting outer results. That does not mean we necessarily will continue in this way, but we do it a lot now. If we start integrating our own inner nature, we need to dive down under, go below or behind the surface and explore in the deep recesses of our nature. There we might discover vast territories and regions full of life. This is not only where we find the subconscious, but we find the superconscious as well.

Realities under or beneath the surface are where reality becomes vast and unfathomable, but it is also where we discover and receive so much insight. Instead of roaming around in the exoteric or outer areas of existence, we dive into the esoteric or inner realms, and here we explore unimagined treasures within ourselves, our ignored or even suppressed nature. It is also here we realize the forgotten people, our close relatives in the planetary wholeness. It has been said that the Sidhe are much more sensitive to starlight than to sunlight. That is also a beautiful fact and a point of reflection. When blazing sunlight is ever present, we cannot experience the darkness of the cosmos and the glittering starlight. The sun simply covers the stars actual existence until the nighttime comes. Then we again sense how we are bathed in magical starlight. If we use this as a metaphor for the difference of human surface-life and the depth-life of the Sidhe, it gives us a good perspective of our need to connect with them.

Into The Zone Of Wonders

Entering into the realm of betwixt and between, the moment after before and before after, right where nothing is ending and everything starts, in the pausing, the in-between, we encounter Sidheness - first of all within us. Right there, presence stirs, and imagination is a here-and-now doorway to that which was never seen before and yet is recognized. Here we become part of the great storytelling, lifted out to the world in song lines that speak to all of us, heart, mind, and body.

The typical human approach can be illustrated by a well-known insight from quantum physics. The smallest physical units are both particles and fields of energy at the same time. The way we approach them determines how they appear. The most prevalent human approach is to experience the world from the particle angle. Compared to this, the dominant Sidhe-approach is definitely the field. We have the saying that we have "a point of view", stressing the particle aspect. The Sidhe in this analogy instead would inhabit the "circumference of awareness", stressing the field aspect. Particles and fields are both true, and we need both to appreciate reality at a deeper level. But humans are very particularized. Isolation grows from a one-sided particle view and reality is fragmented into endless pieces. We deeply need to embrace the field-awareness to plug into the depths of connectedness. Here we can move into the Sidhe-ness in ourselves.

Within us is a vast cosmos awaiting to become conscious. In attempting to do this in the way that brings our inner Sidhe-nature into focus in that greatness, we are less helped by our logical mind than our lyrical perception. It is in our role as life-musicians and creative poets we are called to become creators of newness and renewed life. In this focus we open to a living playfulness and a spontaneity that is full of joy and life-affirmation. Reconnecting to the field of life is an opening to the natural magic in everything, the transforming aliveness that will help us to experience the world as completely new, and to create a world even beyond imagination. To touch the Sidhe-heart in us is to reconnect to innocence and deep caring. It is to rekindle the flame of joy and hope, and to start imagining wonderful possibilities and the deep weaving of all life into the greater symphony gradually unfolding on our planet. Wholeness is at hand, in all its aliveness and up and down is turned around, as AE says in *"A Memory"*, referring to what life may be when we discover the hidden treasures:

*"From the flowers in heaven dancing
To the stars that shine in the grass."*

From this place of wonders, we can rise out of our conscious awareness where we are trapped in oblivion, and realize we need each other to make the world whole again. Our Sidhe-relatives are reaching out, inviting us to a renewed contact with the world and with them. The reason is obvious. The way humans treat the planet today in many ways is so destructive and one-sided that there is no prospect to a better future. That is the reason why Yeats and AE and others came under the influence of the Sidhe and that is exactly why we can go further today. But in order to appreciate where we are today and what we can do, it is important to see who helped prepare the way before us.

The Seers

Ireland owes gratitude to two cultural pioneers who deeply affected the Emerald Isle and the modern Celtic identity. They are known to have spearheaded the Irish Literary Renaissance, but they were also working for Irish independence and cultural significance. The beauty of their lifework is that they both influenced Ireland on different levels – inwardly and outwardly, socially, culturally, and spiritually.

Yeats and AE met each other as teenagers at the Metropolitan School of Art, and one of their teachers was John Butler Yeats, W. B. Yeats' father. During these early years the young men wrote poetry together, became friends, and soon after AE was introduced to Theosophy. This was deeply significant. AE became a member in 1890 and the Theosophical movement, founded by H. P. Blavatsky, would have a deep influence, including that AE married Violet North who was also a Theosophist. As we shall see, through the study of Theosophy Yeats also opened to further engagements with spiritual movements. The two kindred spirits traveled on a trajectory with many similarities as well as many differences.

Both men were seers, each in their way and central to their involvement was a Celtic identity that included the reality of the Sidhe, the Irish Faery Folk. A clear evidence of the significance AE and Yeats had, and of their relationship, is to be found in the famous book from 1911, "*The Fairy-Faith in Celtic Countries*" by W. Y. Evans-Wentz. The author dedicated his heavy volume to none other than "*A.E., whose unwavering loyalty to the fairy-faith has inspired much that I have herein written, whose friendly guidance in my study of Irish mysticism I most gratefully acknowledge; and William Butler Yeats, who brought me at my own Alma Mater in California the first message from Fairyland, and who afterwards in his own country led me through the haunts of Fairy Kings and Queens.*" It is from this perspective they are introduced in the following chapters.

William Butler Yeats
(1865-1939)

Yeats needs no introduction, but one will be offered here anyway as the angle in this book is slightly different from the usual praises he rightfully receives for his cultural pioneering. He is considered to be one of the most influential writers in the 20th century and he was awarded the Nobel Prize in Literature in 1923. His central role in the Irish Literary Revival, also known as *The Celtic Twilight*, is well known and together with many artists and intellectuals he worked to renew the interest in Irish cultural identity through theatre, poetry, mythology, folklore, Gaelic language, dances, music, and song.

Lifelong Occult Involvements

Yeats was an intellectual, but he was also deeply immersed in occult tradition and spiritual mysticism, and this clearly included a focus on the Sidhe. In his early days at the Metropolitan School of Art in Dublin he learned about Theosophy and in 1887 he personally met H. P. Blavatsky, the founder of modern Theosophy. He remained involved in esoteric philosophy and was a seeker and curious investigator into all kinds of questions. In 1890 he joined the Hermetic Order of the Golden Dawn, a highly ritualistic movement occupied with angelic contacts and ceremonial magic. He remained a member of the order for decades. He also became a member of Stella Matutina, another ritualistic order with intricate symbolism. Yeats was clearly attracted to complexity and metaphysical involvement that required much knowledge and studies.

Theosophy is a view of life that involves the belief in reincarnation and karma, dharma, graduated planes of existence, teachings about the evolution and unfoldment of the soul and the personality, descriptions of auras, centers and a wide range of energies that can be perceived by higher sense perception (ESP). It embraces a belief in the existence of spiritual masters, angels, nature spirits and other beings, an understanding of how the world unfolds through different ages of thousands of years, even millennia, and how the planet as a living being goes through different evolutionary stages or kalpas. Everything in the cosmos is considered alive and evolving, from atoms and cells to solar systems and galaxies. Everything is energy, whether it is physical, emotional, mental, soul-related and beyond to the most exalted spiritual conditions. Divinity is perceived as both inherent in creation and transcendent beyond all created forms, subtle or concrete. All religions are seen as describing the same universal reality with different dialects, and art, philosophy and science are considered to be complementary with religion as different languages of the greater reality. Humanity is considered as one family and the vision is that we will finally live in peace all over the globe as we unfold our inherent light, love, and creative power. Theosophy is called occultism because occult means hidden or invisible and much of what Theosophy describes eludes the physical senses and is what would be called paranormal. Yeats embraced this view of existence, plus the ritualistic and ceremonial involvements as expressed in the Golden Dawn and wherever he encountered it.

One of his early works that won him a reputation as a significant poet, was *The Wanderings of Oisin and other poems*. This was right to the core of Irish mythology. Oisin communicates with St. Patrick about his journey to Tír na nÓg, the world of the Faeries or the Sidhe. It is also a love story between the faery princess, Niamh and Oisin. The poem describes how Oisin lived three hundred years in the land of the Sidhe with dance, music, feasting and hunting, having adventures and journeys. Yeats early set the tone for the Sidhe and their place in Irish culture, mythology, and history by weaving the patterns of myth, spirituality, imagination, and outer reality that invited readers into a widening perspective of existence. He was not shy or reserved about his involvements, and it says a lot about the Irish mentality that his fame has not been ridiculed or diminished because of his exploration of these dimensions of life.

Myth And Sidhe

As Yeats was deeply engaged with reviving Irish mythology and the living tradition of faeries or the Sidhe, it is no surprise that he gave his own contribution, not only in poems and written pieces, but also in literary publications like *The Wanderings of Oisin*. The very beginning of the Irish Literary Revival was marked by works he spearheaded, not the least of which is the well-known book, *Fairy and Folk Tales of the Irish Peasantry* in 1888, and later *Irish Fairy Tales*, published in 1892.

For Yeats no doubt he personally was convinced of the reality of the Sidhe, and it was partly based upon personal experiences. It is worth noticing that *The Yeats Society* in Sligo welcomes visitors with the following lines written on the wall of the entrance from Yeats' play, "*The Land of Heart's Desire*" (1894)

"*Faeries, come take me out of this dull world,*
For I would ride with you upon the wind,
Run on the top of the disheveled tide,
And dance upon the mountains like a flame."

The play itself features a faery child that visits humans, shocks the priest, talks about the faery land "*where beauty has no ebb, decay no flood, but joy is wisdom, time and endless song*", and she invites a newlywed woman into her world as she dies. It is significant that of the many quotes *The Yeats Society* could have chosen, a Call to the Sidhe was the invitation selected for visitors.

In "*The Fairy-Faith in the Celtic Countries*" Yeats is asked if he believes in the Celtic Fairy Kingdom. His answer (p. 66) is loud and clear: "*I am certain that it exists and will someday be studied as it was studied by Kirk.*" – referring to Robert Kirk, the Gaelic scholar and folklorist, minister of Aberfoyle in Scotland who wrote "*The Secret Commonwealth*", a treatise on fairy folklore completed in 1692. There is no doubt that Yeats, despite his changing priorities during life, kept a deep conviction in the core truths of Celtic tradition and to this tradition belongs the lore and experiences of the Good People, the Sidhe.

George William Russell
'AE' (1867-1935)

The Irish novelist and poet, James Stephens (1882-1959), said of George William Russell (calling him Æ or AE): *"AE was the most remarkable man I have ever known. To a young man he was alarming, inspiring, astonishing. He was, professionally, a seer, a painter, a poet, an essayist, a journalist, an economist, and with one exception the greatest conversationalist I have ever met. He was just one boundless torrent of energy."* (Marcus Beale, p. 4) This sets the tone for the way AE impressed the people he met. This was a man that deeply influenced so many lives, both with his wide and deep knowledge, his skills, his activism, his balanced patriotism, and his helpfulness towards other people.

George William Russell, known as AE – an abbreviation of Aeon which he symbolically called himself as an artist – was not only a highly active social and cultural pioneer, and a partner with Yeats in the Irish Literary Revival, but was also a mystic and a seer of rare standard. In Ireland he is renowned for being a bold Irish nationalist, a champion for the Irish farmers and a literary critic who found new talents in the Irish literary renaissance. But understanding AE requires a much deeper study into his work as a Theosophist, a mystic, a painter, and not the least – a poet. In many ways, however, he has been in the shadow of his world-famous friend. Considering them as Yin and Yang forces in creating a bridge to the Sidhe, Yeats is the extroverted, eccentric, cultural trailblazer with a sophisticated mind and an intellectual vibe. AE is the more introverted spiritual pioneer who fascinated most people on a deep level when they met him, and who had a shyness about him in spite of his public role.

Justice, Dignity And Humaneness

A main reason for AE's highly respected position in recent Irish history is that he was a practical man, and a pioneer for Irish independence. He became a journalist and an editor and did important work as an economist and assistant secretary for the Irish Agricultural Organization Society (IAOS). He travelled to all counties of Ireland and talked to the farmers about the possibilities and strength if they organized in co-operatives. He revered the farmers and working people and was working hard for their dignity and recognition of their importance. In this way, he supported Irish agriculture and the growing awareness of a modern Irish identity.

In 1905 he became the editor of the Irish Homestead, the important newspaper of the IAOS, and for decades he was deeply involved not only in agriculture, but in many aspects of Irish culture. The Homestead evolved into a central organ giving voice to Irish cultural opinion and literature and as a patriot, AE published international news and helped Ireland in achieving independence. As mentioned, he was also a burning voice for the poor, was against capitalism and its greedy nature, and fought for ordinary people and for real justice. No matter how much he was against injustice, he never forgot the ethical dimension of life. He is known for having said: *"We may fight against what is wrong, but if we allow ourselves to hate, that is to ensure our spiritual defeat and our likeness to what we hate."* ("The Living Torch, A.E", by Monk Gibbon, 1937) This spectrum of social and cultural activities gives a solid background for appreciating AE as a deep, visionary mystic, not as a feeble dreamer but as an accomplished reformer who combined outer obligations with inner explorations.

At the same time AE was deeply committed to Theosophy and metaphysical understanding. For him this interest was a lifelong companionship and a key to his deepest identity. His dedication to Theosophy and his involvement in esoteric spirituality was something he weaved into the rest of his activities with no shyness or reservation. He saw it as belonging to the core of his driving energy. Some years after the death of H. P. Blavatsky, the founder of The Theosophical Society, AE left the organization and focused on reviving The Hermetic Society he once founded with Yeats. The influence of esoteric philosophy runs like a golden thread in his writings and poems, and his spiritual autobiography, *"The Candle of Vision"*, is a powerful testament to this.

Singing With Words And Colors

AE was so clearly a mystic and his approach to the profundity of life was primarily done through poetry and painting. To him words were not just forms, but vehicles that can transport us to the beyond. To him colors were not just pigments and hues but living qualities that convey the facets of life and invite us on an inner journey. He took deep delight in painting, and he said that nature intended him to be a painter. When he painted, he experienced something beginning to glow under his fingers and the very act of molding colors, moods and motives was magical to him. The aesthetic sense and beauty for him were pathways to the divine. Painting affected him profoundly and he was very productive.

Often his paintings were of Donegal with images of sand beaches or forests or mountains, and humans appearing as small beings in the gigantic cathedral of nature. Very often he included portraits of the Sidhe or other nature beings and mythological themes as well. A significant number of AE's paintings portray nude children bathing in the sea, or women and children at sea, or in forests, often playing. It is so clear from the atmosphere in the paintings that innocence and delight is the predominant feature. A certain kind of softness is visible, and AE is very consciously working with the light and with golden hues. This sweetness and joy are a gateway to the Sidhe, and intermingles effortlessly as when he starts his poem *"The Golden Age"*:

"When the morning breaks above us
And the wild sweet stars have fled,
By the faery hands that love us
Wakened you and I will tread."

Writing poems made it possible for him to bring a kind of mantric singing into language. One of his central books istitles "*Songs and its Fountains*", and in it he explores words, language, and imagination. To AE imagination was a doorway to truth, not simply a way of dreaming and having fantasies. Imagination can bring deep visions and AE described many of his profound experiences, several that could be called paranormal including extensive clairvoyant experiences. There is always a rare openness to the magnificence of life in experiencing the facets of one's imagination and AE practiced this with a mind woven into nature, gentleness, and innocence as he says in "*A Summer Night*":

"*Out of its majesty, as child to child.*
I think upon it all with heart grown wild."

The Mighty Mother

Nature to AE was anything other than building materials and resources. Nature is the living expression of the breathing being we are all part of. His admonition would never be that we should seek in heaven what we had found on earth, but the opposite: That we should seek on earth, what we have found in heaven. It is here we live, and it is here the divine mystery of existence is unfolding. We are in the living temple of nature, and that was Mother Earth to him. In the poem "*To the Consecrated*" he says:

"*The Mighty Mother nourished you;*
Her breath blew from her mystic bowers;
Their elfin glimmer floated through
The pureness of your shadowy hours."

Mother Nature is the nourisher, and the elfin glimmer refers to the atmosphere of the Sidhe realm, always behind and permeating our world and the visible natural world. In his poem, "*The Earth Breath*" – clearly referring to the livingness of our entire planet – he pays homage to the divine feminine:

> "*And unto the Mighty Mother,*
> *Gay, eternal, rise*
> *All the hopes we hold, the gladness,*
> *Dreams of things to be.*
> *One of all thy generations,*
> *Mother, hails to thee.*
> *Hail, and hail, and hail forever*"

This is unreservedly an honoring of the Mother as equal to the Father. Incredibly and powerfully asserted, AE is a guardian of the divine feminine, and his approach to nature is to honor and contemplate the livingness and beauty of the manifested divine. But he does not forget the other end of the divine polarity, as when in the poem "The Free" he brings them together with great warmth:

> "*The smile of the dark hidden Father,*
> *The Mother with magical breath.*"

Fairy Cottage

AE had a friendship with the Irish nationalist politician Hugh A. Law (1872-1943), who represented Donegal as a member of Parliament in the United Kingdom House of Commons. He lived in Marble Hill House in the northwestern corner of Ireland with his family, and AE was a family friend. They had originally built a cottage for their children and offered AE an invitation to live in the cottage whenever he visited the area. It became his studio, and he spent a lot of time there walking along the sand beaches in Dunfanaghy, in the wilderness of Hornhead and in nearby places. In a way, it became his artistic refuge, and the magical place became known as Fairy Cottage.

Detail from AE's "Fairy Cottage" Donegal, Ireland

*Artist's note: This is my painting based on a black and white photo of the interior of the Fairy Cottage from AE's time. This may represent "lost" AE art. Color is based on a pallet used in some of AE's Sidhe paintings. JBerg

AE deeply loved Donegal and he perceived it as more than a nice area to visit. In a letter to John Quinn in 1904 he wrote:

"Oh Donegal! It is the spiritual center of Ireland, and the loveliest place on the face of the earth, to me at least...Endless stone walls, hills, lakes, mountains, woods, seas, moons, stars, and people with the kindness of God in their hearts. I used to hesitate between Rosses Point and Dunfanaghy in Donegal but now have plumped for Dunfanaghy and will go there when I die and sit on Breaghy Hill or Angus Head watching the procession of the thoughts of God." (Marcus Beale, p. 19)

Painting and writing were his activities when he was in residence there. He sold quite a few paintings and it supported the income he needed to work for the Agricultural Movement and to be active in its social and cultural activities. But it was not just a means to an end. In an interview for the New York Telegram in 1930 (Marcus Beale, p. 47) he wrote:

"When I go into an Irish valley or climb an Irish hill to paint, it is so different for me, my emotions expand, and my fingers palpitate. Painting is the greatest passion in life for me. There is no escaping it; nor would I care to."

When painting he also wrote poems and letters to friends. The contact with nature was crucial for him. In a letter to Vachel Lindsay in 1931 he mentioned how he could see Mount Muckish from his door in Fairy Cottage:

"I eat griddle bread, drink buttermilk, sit by a turf fire and walk over hills and sands and try to empty my mind so that Mother Earth may come into it and talk to me a little." (Marcus Beale, p. 19)

The Fairy Cottage is still there but is now only an enchanted ruin in the forest behind Marble Hill House, enveloped in the greenness of the forest and not accessible to the public. In a way this magical spot has been given back to the undisturbed wildness just behind Marble Hill beach where an excellent cup of coffee can be enjoyed at The Shack. AE often painted on this beach and it is still possible to hear stories about him from local folks.

AE not only found his sweet spot, but also discovered the magical area of his life where he connected most deeply with nature and the Sidhe. But AE also loved the Sligo area, and it was he who invited Yeats to experience the depth and beauty of Sligo, the very place that now is called Yeats Country. In a letter to Yeats in 1896 AE wrote: *"I wish you could come over to this county Sligo… and absorb this new force. To me enchantment and fairyland are real and no longer dreams."* Letter to W. B. Yeats, 2. February 1896 (Letters from AE, edited by Alan Denson (London, Abelard-Schuman, 1961, p. 18)

Personal Encounters With The Sidhe

Often AE had deep experiences with the Sidhe in all their glory. When he refers to these encounters, he is mostly a spectator to beings of wonder. He never refers to a personal contact, but he is clearly a visitor in their realm. This realm is what Irish tradition has given many names: Plain of Delight, Very Deep (*Annwn*), Multi-colored Place (*Ildathach*), Plane of Delight (*Mag Mell*) or mostly known as, Land of Youth (*Tír na nÓg*). To him the most frequent gateways to the Sidhe were the mountains, the hillsides, and the green, wild nature of Ireland in general, and gateways could also be found at the coast, in forests and at ancient places like Newgrange. Frequently these personal encounters appeared in the background of his paintings and he made numerous portraits and illustrations of the Sidhe, or as he sometimes also called them, the Faery Folk.

In his poem *"Carrowmore"* AE refers to the inner realms

behind our mountains and how this presence is characterized by singing and dancing. He also calls this presence the Land of Youth, the English phrase for Tír na nÓg, the most well-known Gaelic word for the Celtic Otherworld where the Sidhe reside. He speaks with such delight in his rhyming:

"Oh, the great gates of the mountain have
opened once again,
And the sound of song and dancing falls
upon the ears of men,
And the Land of Youth lies gleaming, flushed
with rainbow light and mirth,
And the old enchantment lingers in the
honey-heart of earth."

AE describes one of his more unique encounters in *"The Candle of Vision"* (p. 34) which takes place in nature, probably somewhere in Donegal around Dunfanaghy and Marble Hill beach:

"Once I lay on the sand dunes by the western sea. The air seemed filled with melody. The motion of the wind made a continuous musical vibration. Now and then the silvery sound of bells broke on my ear. I saw nothing for a time. Then there was an intensity of light before my eyes like the flashing of the sunlight through a crystal. It widened like the opening of a gate and I saw the light was streaming from the heart of a glowing figure. Its body was pervaded with light as if sunfire rather than blood ran through its limbs. Light streams flowed from it. It moved over me along the winds, carrying a harp, and there was a circling of golden hair that swept across the strings. Birds flew about it, and over the brows was a fiery plumage as of wings of outspread flame. On the face was an ecstasy of beauty and immortal youth. There were others, a lordly folk, and they passed by on the wind as if they knew me not or the earth I

lived on. When I came back to myself my own world seemed grey and devoid of light though the summer sun was hot upon the sands."

AE makes specific mention of his visions and what they are about: *"And I saw, without being able to explain to myself their relation to that exalted humanity, beings such as the ancient poets described, a divine folk who I think never were human but were those spoken of as the Sidhe."* (p. 165) He also describes an experience where he is shown the four sacred hallows of the Sidhe, a gigantic sword of quivering flame, a great spear, a cauldron, and a glittering stone (p. 167)

In *"The Fairy-Faith in Celtic Countries"* by W. Y. Evans-Wentz (p. 59-66), the author refers to *"An Irish Mystic's Testimony"* with a great deal of reverence. The mystic was AE, but he was anonymous in the book although the manuscript itself was dedicated to him and Yeats. The text is in the form of an interview where AE identified at least two distinct categories: a) The Shining Beings, and b) The Opalescent Beings. The first category seems to be identical with nature spirits, elemental beings, and part of the Devic kingdom with a collective consciousness. The Opalescent Beings on the other hand are clearly individualized and possess an inner light. AE identified them as belonging to *Tuatha de Danaan*.

The Inner Sidhe

It is crucial if we are going to understand AE, to emphasize that he was not only talking about the Sidhe as a people we can meet. He was aware of our inner Sidhe nature, that part of us which we share with them, just as they share their rudimentary human seed with us. In one of his poems, *"The Palaces of the Sidhe"*, he states this clearly in referring to them as catalysts of our own Sidhe-depth:

"The faery folk who are able
To make us faery ourselves."

AE, without doubt, was a profound link to a revival of the knowledge of the Sidhe in Ireland during his lifetime. He went further than Yeats, but together they stand out as a complementary duo in the revival of the Celtic Sidhe awareness. Their poems still have the vibrant vitality and actuality we can be inspired by. So, let us enter the domain of poetry and rhyme.

The Call

The Sidhe are calling us today in increasing numbers, offering us a possible new partnership in the service of wholeness and a new way of healing accumulated scars and the weight and pressure they hold. We are in a deep global crisis and the call is an invitation for us to reconsider our role in the planetary totality. We have developed our global dominance into a gridlock that is choking us and the rest of the planetary home. Gross materialism and greed based on isolation and loss of humility has created heavy pollution, deadly conflicts, extreme poverty, and a deeply challenging climate change forcing us to look at ourselves with seriousness and urgency.

From a completely unexpected angle we are discreetly approached by an ancient relative we have repressed into myth and fantasy to protect ourselves from the fringes of our ancient awareness. In spite of the risks of ridicule and dismissal, there is an attempt from the Sidhe to reach out and invite us to re-build the bridges between us so that together we can help heal the earth. It is a daring enterprise. Yet, it is not entirely new. In the days of Yeats and AE something was growing and taking an initial shape. No matter how scarce and rudimentary it might seem today, its beginnings are worth noting. And more than that - by acknowledging the inspirations that came through and made a difference, we might increase the efforts today and add our own energy to the growing tide. The following poems are examples of pioneering bridges that helped bring forth the momentum that is growing today. However, these poems are also available in the here and now with their freshness, and they may surprise us in their partly timeless nature and poetic innocence. Although Yeats has been acknowledged over time, have his poems been understood yet? And what about AE? Are the days of his deeper impact finally here now?

The Song of Wandering Aengus

This poem is one of the most well-known poems of Yeats, appearing in *"The Wind Among the Reeds"* from 1899. It is on the top five list of the most popular poems of Ireland. The title itself refers to Aengus, the Celtic god associated with youth, love, and inspiration. He is one of the Tuatha Dé Danann and there are many stories about him in Celtic mythology. In one of the tales, *"The Dream of Oengus"*, he fell in love with a girl he had seen in his dreams - said to be the most beautiful girl in Ireland. Approaching him, she suddenly vanished but kept coming back to play and sing for him, then disappeared again night after night in a mysterious way. His parents, god Dagda and the goddess Boann of the River Boyne where Newgrange is situated, searched for a long time to find the girl, but failed. They had to call out to the fairy king of Munster, who found the maiden after a yearlong search, and Aengus was brought to the place where she was. He recognized her and easily picked her out from a group of 150 maidens. However, he found out that the girl and the maidens changed into the shape of birds every second year, so he shapeshifted into a swan and together, as two white birds, they were united.

The very idea of shapeshifting is at the core of the Sidhe tradition, but it is also a reminder of the universal qualities of Gods and immortal beings in many traditions. The Greek Zeus shapeshifted into forms like a swan and a white bull while he fertilized women and multiplied his presence in the world. The renowned British bard, Taliesin, shapeshifted into a hare, a fish, a bird, and a piece of grain on his journey of transformation into the bard he became.

Yeats seems to use exactly the mythical story of the dream of Aengus and transforms it into a tale to be told in verse. The story is a vivid memory that comes alive by a young man who encounters a glimmering girl emerging and transforming from a trout he caught in a stream. In Yeats' poem the transformation is the presence of a Sidhe emerging from a trout and connecting with a young man in a special way. She calls him by his name.

To be called by one's name is something incredibly unique – it is personal. Assuming that our name is a symbol of the essence of our identity, this encounter between the girl and the young man is an intimate meeting of identities. Something is stirred.

And now the old man looks back and remembers the magical encounter. In all the years of his life he has not been able to find the enchanting girl of his youth. She disappeared like a mist in the air. But, he has not given up. He will continue his wanderings until he finds her, kisses her, and holds her hand as they walk in the grass and pluck silver and golden apples of the moon and the sun. There is a deep longing in the poem, a longing for reunion, for reconnecting with magic and deep identity. This makes the lines incredibly special as a falling in love between Sidhe and Humanity and a possible promise that someday silver and gold might come together again.

The Song of Wandering Aengus

I went out to the hazel wood
Because a fire was in my head
And I cut and peeled a hazel wand
And hooked a berry with a thread

And when white moths were on the wing
And moth-like stars were flickering out
I dropped a berry in a stream
And caught a little silver trout.

When I had laid it on the floor
I went to blow the fire aflame
But something rustled on the door
And someone called me by my name.

It had become a glimmering girl
With apple blossoms in her hair
Who called me by my name and ran
And faded through the brightening air.

Though I am old with wandering
Through hollow lands and hilly lands
I will find out where she has gone
And kiss her lips and take her hands

And walk among long dappled grass
And pluck till time and times are done
The silver apples of the moon,
The golden apples of the sun.

The Stolen Child

"The Stolen Child" is an epic poem from Yeats' hand, written in 1886 and widely known all around the world. It has been put to music by many notable artists, including Cyril Rootham, The Waterboys, Loreena McKennitt, Steve Hackett from Genesis, and Eric Whitacre. It has also been used in films, for instance in Steven Spielberg's "*A.I. Artificial Intelligence*" where the chorus of the poem appears.

The poem goes right to the core of Irish tradition and the storytelling about the Sidhe, also called Faeries. The theme is traditionally interpreted as the story of abduction. In several lands there has been the admonition surrounding Faeries that humans should be careful not to engage with them as they risk snatching children away, becoming changelings or losing their minds. A changeling is a word for an entity taking over the body of a person, and losing one's mind means being lost to rationality and normality – two scary scenarios making the Faeries dangerous creatures not to be approached. Often the stories of Faeries or Sidhe have this eerie atmosphere of danger and warnings and it is easy to understand why. Encountering the so-called unknown equals, stepping out of our comfort-zone, and admonitions like this becomes preventive precautions, a protective strategy to deal with the alien world outside our well-known human civilization.

However, nothing seems to suggest that the Faeries in Yeats' poem are deceptive, seductive or beguiling creatures. On the contrary, it is a much deeper story from his hand, and it is a rescue operation. If we think about the child as a universal metaphor for our unspoiled innocence, our inner child, this really becomes the story about how we can save our inherent goodness in a troubled world full of suffering and pain. Instead of giving in to the toughness of modern jungle consciousness and surrendering to brutality and alienation, we can take refuge in the place where 'the waters and the wild' reside. We can do that by answering the invitation from the Sidhe, taking their hand and letting them help us reconnect with nature and the natural way of being in the world. It will bring us true renewal and a freeing from business as usual. To the comfort-seeking people this might feel like something frightening and deeply unnatural, but for the individuals longing for regeneration and a new vision for the future, it might be the saving grace.

Yeats' close friend, AE, also supported this version of what the poem is all about. He made a painting that clearly seems to visualize the poem lucidly. The painting's title is "*The Stolen Child*" and today, it is part of the Trinity Art Collection in Dublin. It depicts a peaceful scenery in nature, held in light bluish colors, where a small child is attended by three gentle, adult presences in white robes with saint-like halos around their heads. The painting radiates care and protection and is a strong clue to the intention of Yeats. There is no hint of abduction or child snatching – on the contrary, the scenery emanates peace and safety.

The poem mentions several places in the Sligo area of northwestern Ireland that are related to faery lore and encounters with the hidden people. Sleuth Wood, today known as Slish Wood, is situated East of Sligo at Lough Gill and was an ancient oak woodland. Its beautiful location between the lake and the Ox Mountains is enriched by a special biodiversity and it is not difficult to sense how this area has been connected to Sidhe encounters. Rosses Point is another area just outside Sligo where Yeats and his family spent time and is also a place of recorded Sidhe encounters. Yeats often referred to the Sidhe in the area and confirmed that he himself had taken part in unusual experiences where the Sidhe could be seen and also heard wonderful music like cathedral bells. The Glencar Waterfall is yet another spectacle in nature that Yeats mentions in the poem. The spectacular beauty of this place and its surroundings is a story in itself. When visiting the waterfall, the mountains behind the falls and the nearby lake offer a truly revelatory experience. The wandering water from the hills above invites a walk into the wild remoteness where an even higher waterfall can be found if hikers leave the designated tracks and follow the sound of the rushing water.

The poem tells the reader or listener that the faeries offer the child "*vats full of berries and of reddest stolen cherries*". In Yeats' time rich fruits like this would have been something special, and stolen cherries indicate not only the idea of "*forbidden fruit*", but also the carefully selected gifts being offered to the child. When we eat something that is offered, we become partakers in the realm we are in. The child is invited to participate in the ancient dances, jumping and holding hands, full of merriment as an antidote and cure against the sufferings and worries of the human world and offered a deep refreshment. The child leaves the well-known everyday life and its "*boiling kettle*" on the hub, and enters the world of "*the waters and the wild*" hand-in-hand with the faeries. The invitation is completed with the actual response by the child who follows the faeries. The child is called "*The solemn-eyed*", truly a reference to depth and sagacity, and not to a naive child being abducted.

The Stolen Child

Where dips the rocky highland
Of Sleuth Wood in the lake,
There lies a leafy island
Where flapping herons wake
The drowsy water rats;
There we've hid our faery vats,
Full of berrys
And of reddest stolen cherries.
Come away, O human child!
To the waters and the wild
With a faery, hand in hand,
For the world's more full of weeping
than you can understand.

Where the wave of moonlight glosses
The dim gray sands with light,
Far off by furthest Rosses
We foot it all the night,
Weaving olden dances
Mingling hands and mingling glances
Till the moon has taken flight;
To and fro we leap
And chase the frothy bubbles,
While the world is full of troubles
And anxious in its sleep.
Come away, O human child!
To the waters and the wild
With a faery, hand in hand,
For the world's more full of weeping
than you can understand.

Where the wandering water gushes
From the hills above Glen-Car,
In pools among the rushes
That scarce could bathe a star,
We seek for slumbering trout
And whispering in their ears
Give them unquiet dreams;
Leaning softly out
From ferns that drop their tears
Over the young streams.
Come away, O human child!
To the waters and the wild
With a faery, hand in hand,
For the world's more full of weeping
than you can understand.

Away with us he's going,
The solemn-eyed:
He'll hear no more the lowing
Of the calves on the warm hillside
Or the kettle on the hob
Sing peace into his breast,
Or see the brown mice bob
Round and round the oatmeal chest.
For he comes, the human child,
To the water and the wild
With a faery, hand in hand,
For the world's more full of weeping
than he can understand.

A Faery Song

A comment to this poem says that this was a *"song by the people of Faery over Diarmuid and Grania, in their bridal sleep under a Cromlech."* This indicates that it was song for a couple, actually a legendary couple in Irish tradition, the stunningly beautiful Lady Grania or Grainne, and her lover Diarmuid. In the well-known story, the couple goes through many sufferings and they are on a long journey to escape. Grainne is daughter of the High King of Ireland and she flees with her lover Diarmuid, a great warrior, to avoid being married to a much older man. The couple is on the run across Ireland for years where they hide in caves, trees, and in all kinds of meager and remote places. Many things happen to them in different versions of the adventure.

Finally, she becomes pregnant and shortly thereafter a tragedy ends their long escape. Close to Ben Bulben, the Faery Fort in County Sligo, Diarmuid fights and kills a wild boar with his sword but is fatally wounded while protecting Grainne from the animal. This story is the plot of a play by Yeats and George Moore from 1901 with music by the English composer, Edward Elgar.

In this haunting poem Yeats let the Sidhe themselves speak. In the play they sing to the couple as they lie in their sleep on their escape under a cromlech, a stone circle with a stone house in the center. Such a place is a typical gateway to the world of the Sidhe, so it is no surprise that the Faery song arises right here. But as the story is the universal, human love story, it also becomes the story of all humans who strive to live and love despite all kinds of dangers. It can be seen as a universal hope or wish from the Sidhe towards humanity.

In his imaginative creativity – or in letting the Sidhe flow through him – Yeats shares an intention from the Sidhe to us. They wish to help us untangle from the weariness and heaviness we experience in our way of living, striving and suffering. They bestow us the gifts of silence, love, starlight, and deep restoration far from our human turmoil.

This blessing is given from the old ones, the joyful ones, the ancient ones, as the Sidhe in their realm live much longer lives than we do in our world. They experience thousands of years in their lives and from their larger perspective they want to help us to experience more freedom and lightness.

There is a deep longing in the poem, like a cry attempting to bridge huge distances. We seem separated from the Sidhe, yet they reach out to us, and there is a hope that something significant may come out of this liberation. Can anything be better and more relevant than peaceful silence, real love, and renewed energy for us today?

So, this really is a Faery song, but it is a reminder to all of us in its haunting simplicity. The message comes through not only in the words, but also in the rhythm and intensity of the sentences, and the way they are repeated. So, here it is:

A Faery Song

We who are old, old and gay,
O so old!
Thousands of years, thousands of years,
If all were told:
Give to these children, new from the world,
Silence and love;
And the long dew-dropping hours of the night,
And the stars above:
Give to these children, new from the world,
Rest far from men.
Is anything better, anything better?
Tell us it then:
Us who are old, old and gay,
O so old!
Thousands of years, thousands of years,
If all were told.

The Hosting of the Sidhe

This poem is steeped in Irish mythology, and it is easy to be carried away from its powerful message by the Celtic names. So, we need to decipher these names to dive into the layers of its meaning.

Knocknarea is a high hill of more than 1000 feet west of Sligo city. At its summit lies Queen Maeve's cairn, one of Ireland's largest. Queen Maeve is a semi-mythical Warrior Queen and full of female power. *Clooth-na bare* is Yeats' dramatically changed name for Cailleach Bhéirre, meaning 'veiled one' and often referred to as 'old woman'. She is a mythical figure of supernatural powers known to have created large hills and mountains, and is associated with Carrowmore at Knocknarea. *Caolte*, (Caílte) is an Irish hero and also a mythological figure and friend of the famous Oisín, Ireland's greatest poet in legend. Caolte is known as a storyteller and for his ability to communicate with animals and move extremely swiftly, again displaying supernatural features. *Niamh*, a fairy woman 'of the golden hair', is also a mythological character and one of the daughters of the god of the sea. Together with Oisín she is a main figure of a famous legend involving a journey to Tír na nÓg, the land of youth or the Sidhe realm.

Yeats played with these mythical identities of power, identifying them with Knocknarea, a place related to the Sidhe. They invite the listener on a journey that could be expressed something like this:

"Let go of your attachments to the outer world of forms. Be free to move – Follow the wild wind. We the Sidhe are in the cold freshness, our hair is blowing in the unfettered wind. We breathe in freedom; we see with clarity. Unimpeded we inhale and exhale - we are in flow."

Then they admonish something that could be seen as a warning for the unprepared and an invitation for the prepared. The Sidhe say that if a person disturbs or impacts their movement, they will stand between the person and what they hope and do. It could be seen as a warning, but it is also an invitation because they are active in the in-between ('twixt night and day). The Sidhe are often present and approachable in the times of dawn and dusk, and what can be better than this? We can also enter the magical realms where things transform if we dare. We are invited to the in-betweenness where the Sidhe are active. Traditionally, the Sidhe are associated with the wind, with whirling winds especially, signifying flow and transformation. As flow dancers we may meet the Sidhe in the in-between if we dare. They call us and invite us to follow them if we dare.

Note: Painting on page 46 by Deva Berg.

The Hosting of the Sidhe

The host is riding from Knocknarea
And over the grave of Clooth-na bare;
Caolte tossing his burning hair
And Niamh calling Away, come away:
Empty your heart of its mortal dream.
The winds awaken, the leaves whirl round,
Our cheeks are pale, our hair is unbound,
Our breasts are heaving, our eyes are agleam,
Our arms are waving, our lips are apart;
And if any gaze on our rushing band,
We come between him and the deed of his hand,
We come between him and the hope of his heart.
The host is rushing 'twixt night and day,
And where is there hope or deed as fair?
Caolte tossing his burning hair,
And Niamh calling Away, come away.

Alter Ego

In this poem AE reminds and invites the reader to experience the Sidhe as the divine Alter Ego, the deeper identity of a person. He shares this in the form of the Fairy lover (Gaelic: *Leanan Sidhe*) but focuses on more than the traditional lore. AE clearly sees the Fairy lover as the inner Sidhe-nature, the spirit of life itself, and therefore the source of inspiration and renewal.

Usually a mortal human being, likely a man, falls deeply in love with an immortal or supernatural Sidhe, most often, a female. This results in a relationship between the Sidhe and the Human – a love affair or even a marriage. In traditional lore there often is a broken promise and a loss of the loved one. The loss sometimes ends with a reunion, and sometimes not. Often poets are said to have been consumed by the fire from the Sidhe - that their love is intense but short. And sometimes the Leanan Sidhe is depicted almost as a vampire, sucking the lifeblood from a bewitched human.

As is so often seen with Yeats and especially AE, the traditional dimension is lifted to another level. We are on an adventure, and it is the hide and seek of life. We are not caught up in the lore that easily gives way to superstition and religious fear, but instead we are moving from a symbolic interpretation to an inner reality. The Fairy lover is the forgotten identity, the Alter Ego we are seeking in order to become whole again. On the life-journey our inner Sidhe-nature can be contacted, sometimes in sleep and sometimes in meditation or through contact with nature. There is innocence similar to when children play, and it is as if life itself whispers that the inner Sidhe – the Fairy lover – and the human being, are one reality and are not separated. Yet, there is loss as this oneness has been forgotten: "We *are one yet know it not*". As in beauty or in a song, there is the possibility to regain contact: "*I to lose myself in thee*".

Alter Ego

All the morn a spirit gay
Breathes within my heart a rhyme,
'Tis but hide and seek we play
In and out the courts of time.

Fairy lover, when my feet
Through the tangled woodland go,
'Tis thy sunny fingers fleet
Fleck the fire dews to and fro.

In the moonlight grows a smile
Mid its rays of dusty pearl—
'Tis but hide and seek the while,
As some frolic boy and girl.

When I fade into the deep
Some mysterious radiance showers
From the jewel-heart of sleep
Through the veil of darkened hours.

Where the ring of twilight gleams
Round the sanctuary wrought,
Whispers haunt me—in my dreams
We are one yet know it not.

Some for beauty follow long
Flying traces; some there be
Seek thee only for a song:
I to lose myself in thee.

On a Hillside

In this poem AE invites us directly into the Sidhe realm through a mountain. This was a frequent passage AE used himself when he had some of his most important Sidhe encounters. He walked in nature often on the hillsides, and meditating there brought him into deep contact with the heart of the mountains. In a small text called *"The Mountains"* written in 1896 for *The Irish Theosophist*, AE mentions certain places in Ireland and says: *"These mountains are sacred in our Celtic traditions. Haunt of the mysteries, here the Tuatha de Danaans once had their home."* Remembering that Tuatha de Danaan is an Irish name for the Sidhe, he actually points to the mountains as their abode. He surely knows they were not only there in the past but also in the present as he had encounters with them in the wilderness. He ends the text by bursting out in poetic rhyming and talks about turning back "mad from the mystic mountains" bubbling with faery gold.

This could be an introduction to the poem *"On a Hillside"* where he shares with the reader how he knows a friendly mountain and his soul is deeply connected to its heart. The hills are doorways to the deep magic and there are halls within them. Here the royal presences can be met, and the visitor can find themselves sitting upon a throne, watching Sirius, the great star above, witnessing white and opal-colored glories. But the visit to the heart of the mountain only lasts a night and then the traveler must return to the grey world above. And even though only faint memories of the visit remain, these are more important than anything the world can offer. Here AE uses sleep as an image of how these realms can be experienced, but for himself, it was a reality accessible in meditation.

There is such a gentleness in the poem. It is like a tender affair between a human and a mountain, a living part of Gaia. But the mountain is also a gateway to a sacred heartland where secrets are to be shared. We are not told the secrets in the poem, but the atmosphere is like an introduction to something immense.

On a Hillside

A friendly mountain I know;
As I lie on the green slope there
It sets my heart in a glow
And closes the door on care.

A thought I try to frame—
I was with you long ago.
My soul from your heart out-came;
Mountain, is that not so?

Take me again, dear hills,
Open the door to me
Where the magic murmur thrills
The halls I do not see,

The halls and caverns deep;
Though sometimes I may dare
Down the twilight stairs of sleep
To meet the kingly there.

Sometimes on flaming wings
I sit upon a throne
And watch how the great star swings
Along the sapphire zone.

It has wings of its own for flight,
Diamond its pinions strong,
Glories of opal and white,
I watch the whole night long.

Until I needs must lay
My royal robes aside
To toil in a world of grey,
Grey shadows by my side.

And when I ponder it o'er
Grey memories only bide,
But their fading lips tell more
Than all the world beside.

The Dream of the Children

This poem is perhaps AE's longest "Sidhe-epos" – an entire "fairy tale" in itself. It unfolds the story of children visiting deep into the majestic mountains. The children are always a reminder of our inner child, so we are invited, and the story is for us. AE reveals quite a bit here. He is generous and poetry can appear so free of the ordinary world that we are not burdened with everyday responsibilities. However, there is much shared, and the hints can be taken further should we choose to accept the invitation.

Essentially, the story tells about children who wake up during their dreaming and experience an entirely different world. Usually walking on the hillsides can be a lonely affair, but now they are suddenly in extremely good company. They are together with the Good People. All the way down into the mountain they sink, listening to music from the mountain's heart. Rainbow colors glitter and there is the presence of an opal star. They are together with opal-colored faery folk wearing tiaras with feathers of starlight. And the magical faeries share some of their secret art with the children. The mountain itself is a blazing fountain and not at all a solid rock. The Sidhe blew the darkness out of the land with their magic and presence – an upliftment in itself. And the children were shown who they really are and called by ancient names. They were told that they could grow into anything they could imagine and help the world come to peace. And when the children came back and woke up to daylight, half of it was forgotten, but half was still with them.

Knowing our true names are like unlocking the doors to our secret heart. We belong to creation not just to an alienated humanity that has forgotten its place in wholeness. The sacred meeting with the Sidhe in the realm of the inner mountains is a chance to remember again, and to take upon ourselves the mantle of Gaian Guardianship. We are called to do this, and in the innocent imagery of children meeting 'the Good People', we are gently asked to become builders of the bridges between worlds so Earth can be healed and become whole again.

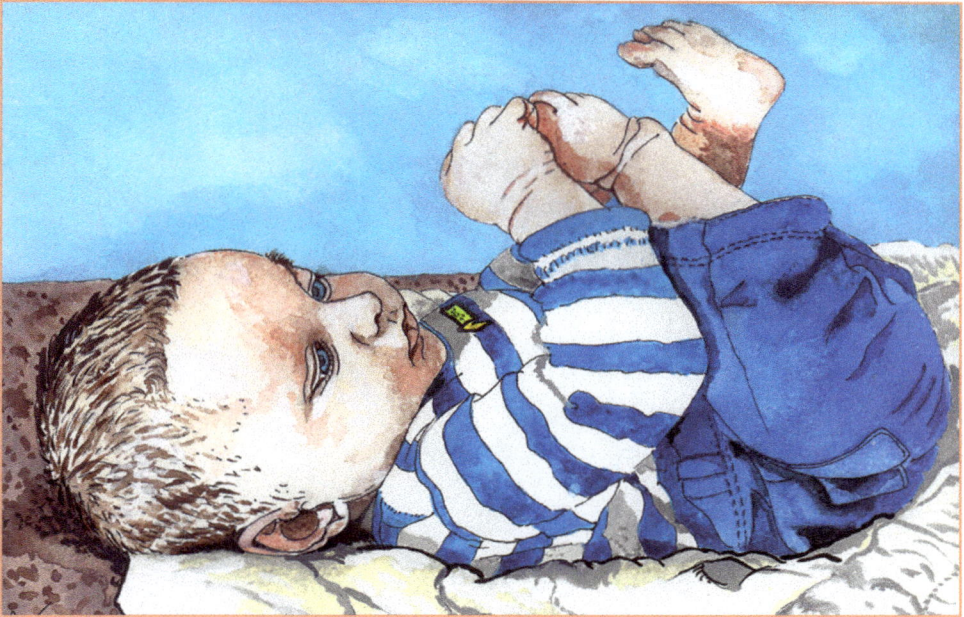

The Dream of the Children

The children awoke in their dreaming
While earth lay dewy and still:
They followed the rill in its gleaming
To the heart-light of the hill.

Its sounds and sights were forsaking
The world as they faded in sleep,
When they heard a music breaking
Out from the heart-light deep.

It ran where the rill in its flowing
Under the star-light gay,
With wonderful color was glowing
Like the bubbles they blew in their play.

From the misty mountain under
Shot gleams of an opal star.
Its pathways of rainbow wonder
Rayed to their feet from afar.

From their feet as they strayed in the meadow
It led through caverned aisles,
Filled with purple and green light and shadow
For mystic miles on miles.

The children were glad: it was lonely
To play on the hillside by day.
"But now," they said, "we have only
To go where the good people stray."

For all the hillside was haunted
By the faery folk come again;
And down in the heart-light enchanted
Were opal-coloured men.

They moved like kings unattended
Without a squire or dame,
But they wore tiaras splendid
With feathers of starlight flame.

They laughed at the children over
And called them into the heart.
"Come down here, each sleepless rover;
We will show you some of our art."

And down through the cool of the mountain
The children sank at the call,
And stood in a blazing fountain
And never a mountain at all.

The lights were coming and going
In many a shining strand,
For the opal fire-kings were blowing
The darkness out of the land.

This golden breath was a madness
To set a poet on fire;
And this was a cure for sadness,
And that the ease of desire.

They said as dawn glimmered hoary,
"We will show yourselves for an hour."
And the children were changed to a glory
By the beautiful magic of power.

The fire-kings smiled on their faces
And called them by olden names,
Till they towered like the starry races
All plumed with the twilight flames.

They talked for a while together
How the toil of ages oppressed,
And of how they best could weather
The ship of the world to its rest.

The dawn in the room was straying:
The children began to blink,
When they heard a far voice saying
"You can grow like that if you think."

The sun came in yellow and gay light:
They tumbled out of the cot:
And half of the dream went with daylight
And half was never forgot.

A New World

This poem by AE is a celebration of the Earth and of life here and now. It is a joyful affirmation and a *Yes!* to being in the present and being in the realm of the sacred Earth, the Mighty Mother. It is also about discovering how the manifested world is also the faery land – a land we also belong to. It is literally brimming with upliftment as it changes the focus from the Otherworld to the experienced reality of the present. The wonder and beauty of creation is right in front of us, and it is in the depths of the Earth. He talks about the mountains as brown breasts full of faery dew. Day and evening are celebrated. Twilight and night are celebrated. The bounty and delicacy of nature is celebrated. And then the poem culminates in a declaration of wonder to the amazing discovery that what we longed for above, is actually below.

In the core of a planet glows a sun so bright that it can make the blaze of the sun at noon less radiant. This is a reverence to Gaia and the manifested world and a reversal of the usual order. AE ends the poem with a gladness of heart as he takes on the dignity of the ancient ones and accepts the mantle of silver mists and golden brightness. There is an echo of the words of Yeats at the end of *"The Song of Wandering Aengus"*, a bringing together of the yin and yang within life.

If there is a poem by AE that sets the scene of affirming the sacredness of Earth, and the mentality that the Sidhe are permeated with, it is this poem. Perhaps that is also why he so clearly calls it *"A New World"* – the dawning of a new era into which we are invited to take part. In a very special way AE is ahead of his time in writing this poem, and perhaps the new era is now. Perhaps this is also why no words are needed but his own:

A New World

I who had sought afar from earth
The faery land to meet,
Now find content within its girth
And wonder nigh my feet.

To-day a nearer love I choose
And seek no distant sphere;
For aureoled by faery dews
The dear brown breasts appear.

With rainbow radiance come and go
The airy breaths of day;
And eve is all a pearly glow
With moonlit winds a-play.

The lips of twilight burn my brow,
The arms of night caress:
Glimmer her white eyes drooping now
With grave old tenderness.

I close mine eyes from dream to be
The diamond-rayed again,
As in the ancient hours ere we
Forgot ourselves to men.

And all I thought of heaven before
I find in earth below:
A sunlight in the hidden core
To dim the noonday glow.

And with the earth my heart is glad,
I move as one of old;
With mists of silver I am clad
And bright with burning gold.

The Palaces Of The Sidhe

AE continues to return to the mountains and to the imagery of children entering them during sleep. He emphasizes the tradition that mountains are places where the Sidhe abide and that beneath the surface of the visible world there are places where the Sidhe live. Several times he describes these as palaces and in this early poem from September 1896, he sets the scene for another journey, not to Australia, yet it is down under and full of wonder! It is like a children's fairy tale, and could easily have been made into a small, illustrated book in itself.

We follow two children with dark and blue eyes and as they leave town to meet the people of wonder, discover their names are Aileen and Rory. It is important to note that the Sidhe or elves or faery folk, as AE calls them, can make us into faeries too – the Sidhe have certain skills and with their help we can somehow replicate those skills in order to enter their world. In this poem, it is through the help of an old man who calls the children "star-hearts" that they are invited into and enter "the elfin land".

They witness a chanting choir and see kings of the faery races sitting on thrones. The palace walls glowed like stars, and they witnessed the initiation of a hero. With chanting and a fire-baptism he is awakened in a pillar of opal glory, and he radiates the faery nature like the others. After this wonderful display, the children are back home, awakened and astonished. They find the place where they entered, but now the rock is solid again and the doorway to the magical land is closed.

Painting from the Card Deck of the Sidhe

The Palaces Of The Sidhe

Two small sweet lives together
From dawn till the dew falls down,
They danced over rock and heather
Away from the dusty town.

Dark eyes like stars set in pansies,
Blue eyes like a hero's bold--
Their thoughts were all pearl-light fancies,
Their hearts in the age of gold.

They crooned o'er many a fable
And longed for the bright-capped elves,
The faery folk who are able
To make us faery ourselves.

A hush on the children stealing
They stood there hand in hand,
For the elfin chimes were pealing
Aloud in the underland.

And over the grey rock sliding,
A fiery colour ran,
And out of its thickness gliding
The twinkling mist of a man--

To-day for the children had fled to
An ancient yesterday,
And the rill from its tunnelled bed too
Had turned another way.

Then down through an open hollow
The old man led with a smile:
"Come, star-hearts, my children, follow
To the elfin land awhile."

The bells above them were hanging,
Whenever the earth-breath blew
It made them go clanging, clanging,
The vasty mountain through.

But louder yet than the ringing
Came the chant of the elfin choir,
Till the mountain was mad with singing
And dense with the forms of fire.

The kings of the faery races
Sat high on the thrones of might,
And infinite years from their faces
Looked out through eyes of light.

And one in a diamond splendour
Shone brightest of all that hour,
More lofty and pure and tender,
They called him the Flower of Power.

The palace walls were glowing
Like stars together drawn,
And a fountain of air was flowing
The primrose colour of dawn.

"Ah, see!" said Aileen sighing,
With a bend of her saddened head
Where a mighty hero was lying,
He looked like one who was dead.

"He will wake," said their guide, "'tis but seeming,
And, oh, what his eyes shall see
I will know of only in dreaming
Till I lie there still as he."

They chanted the song of waking,
They breathed on him with fire,
Till the hero-spirit outbreaking,
Shot radiant above the choir.

Like a pillar of opal glory
Lit through with many a gem--
"Why, look at him now," said Rory,
"He has turned to a faery like them!"

The elfin kings ascending
Leaped up from the thrones of might,
And one with another blending
They vanished in air and light.

The rill to its bed came splashing
With rocks on the top of that:
The children awoke with a flashing
Of wonder, "What were we at?"

They groped through the reeds and clover--
"What funny old markings: look here,
They have scrawled the rocks all over:
It's just where the door was: how queer!"

A Call Of The Sidhe

The Faeries are out – the Sidhe are here! AE's compelling poem describes the Faery children leaving their mountain dwelling at twilight, and filling the air with their joyful songs and sharing their faery stories. In this enchanted world rivers of faery light flow, full of silver flames from the stars that light up the darkness. There is an ecstasy in the air, and we are invited to join the Faery children - they are the voice of the Earth. We are also invited to Tír na nÓg, the Land of Youth, the Sidhe realm, where the trees are heavy with starry fruits. We are invited to drink the nectar that will quench our deepest longing and renew us so that we can unfold our starry nature here on Earth. This call of the Sidhe is not just an invitation from AE, it is what is happening even today. We are invited into a renewed life and the Sidhe are our helpers in this wonderful endeavor and exploration. Listen to AE's inspired voice and rhyme and sense the reverberation of our Sidhe friends behind his poetic intention.

A Call Of The Sidhe

Tarry thou yet,
late lingerer in the twilight's glory:
Gay are the hills with song:
earth's faery children leave
More dim abodes to roam
the primrose-hearted eve,
Opening their glimmering lips
to breathe some wondrous story.
Hush, not a whisper!
Let your heart alone go dreaming.
Dream unto dream may pass:
deep in the heart alone
Murmurs the Mighty One
his solemn undertone.
Canst thou not see adown
the silver cloudland streaming
Rivers of faery light,
dewdrop on dewdrop falling,
Star-fire of silver flames,
lighting the dark beneath?
And what enraptured hosts
burn on the dusky heath!
Come thou away with them
for Heaven to Earth is calling.
These are Earth's voice
—her answer—spirits thronging.
Come to the Land of Youth:
the trees grown heavy there
Drop on the purple wave
the starry fruit they bear.

Drink: the immortal waters
quench the spirit's longing.
Art thou not now, bright one,
all sorrow past, in elation,
Made young with joy,
grown brother-hearted with the vast,
Whither thy spirit wending
flits the dim stars past
Unto the Light of Lights
in burning adoration.

The Future

From the enchanting poems and the deep wisdom of these two Irish trailblazers, we will make a giant leap into our time and open to perspectives for the future. Where are we now, and what may lie ahead when we contemplate the rare gifts from the past? Recent years have seen a revival of the Sidhe in a modern context. The rich contributions of David Spangler and Jeremy Berg have shown a new trajectory for the Sidhe-Human relationship, and significant teachers such as John Matthews and R.J. Stewart are bringing meaningful aspects into the equation. I warmly recommend exploring all of these vital contributions more deeply. In fact, a growing number of individuals are sharing important inspiration in their awareness and connection to the Sidhe, and the diversity is encouraging and shows signs of a healthy and promising new wave. In the following, I offer a contribution to what could be considered core themes describing where we are and how we can move into a more whole, harmonious, and healthy world.

From Adoration To Partnership

It is abundantly clear that AE in particular had a deep communion with the Sidhe-nature, not only in his encounters but also in his own conscious awareness. There are many necessary and deeply needed qualities woven into his writings - from almost ecstatic joyful states to realizations of connectedness, livingness, beauty, and majestic greatness. These are among the most treasured gifts he, and to a certain extent Yeats, bring to the reader and participants in the Sidhe realm. AE also offers intriguing descriptions, sometimes written and sometimes painted, of the inherent nature of the Sidhe which can be of help to anyone interested in this world and its vast possibilities for us.

At the same time, we are, in a peculiar way, invited as

spectators to something that is unfolding at a certain distance. Neither AE or Yeats – to our knowledge – had individual communication with the Sidhe in ways we know of today. They experienced the Sidhe mostly as transcendent beings of an extremely exalted nature which contributed to their experiences of being lifted up into different planes of being. They each described the sense of experiencing something bordering the unattainable, and presented a mixture of Gaelic, mythical gods, and advanced beings. The tone was idealistic and romantic, and clearly served the purpose of bringing the Sidhe and our inner Sidhe-ness into focus as something forgotten and desirable. Our attention is drawn towards something important. But there was also a lack of equality and a level playing field that today would act as a hindrance for a realistic approach.

What we need in our situation is communication and an exchange that brings us into a partnership with the Sidhe - not adoration and devotion that can easily create glamor and twisted proportions. The Sidhe are not gods or immortals. They are close relatives to us, and a partnership with them is crucial if we are to heal the world from the most damaging scars humanity has created. This is a central element of what we need today. At the same time, it is important that we truly honor the legacy of these two wise pioneers and especially the Irish people and lore. Partnership means multiple things and some of this is shared in the following narrative.

The Second Innocence

What is obvious, both for Yeats and AE, is how central they place childhood, youth, and innocence within the Sidhe perspective. "*The Stolen Child*" and "*The Dream of the Children*" are clear examples emphasizing precious human qualities that call for our fullhearted care. Although we could easily dismiss their writings as superficial children's stories, that would miss the whole point. Everything relating to the nature of the child is a reminder of our inner child or the child within us, the part of us that easily ends up being marginalized or even heavily suppressed or damaged. We desperately need the part of us that unfolds in our early years, particularly in a world that focuses so one-sidedly on adult skills and on living in a world for serious, rational grownups. This is not a small detail. Perhaps more than anything, this is the elephant in the room when we consider the good life.

Our childhood represents our first innocence. The second innocence is what emerges when we reclaim it in the adult world, often against all odds. What we need to realize is that without our second innocence, the future of the world will be more than miserable and even gloomy. We are up against cynicism and cold-heartedness and a materialistic, rigid, mechanical mentality that dominates most of the world. It can look foolish and hopelessly unrealistic to insist on warm and soft values in an age where money and image often talks louder than kindness and a humane approach to all challenges. However, there is a desperate need to go beyond this zombie-like rationale that has possessed the zeitgeist of this time. We need the redeeming influence of the liberating and life-affirming second innocence in the adult sphere of life.

The Sidhe dimension can be likened to a much longed for soul-massage and a deeply needed felt sense of embodiment. The second innocence is like breathing again after having barely survived in a toxic environment, and it can be seen in the need for empathy, presence, and the qualities of being rather than of doing. We humans need to rediscover our deep humaneness. When we start doing that, sooner or later, we will stumble upon the overlooked, magical gem – the hidden ElvenHeart in our innermost sanctuary.

Rewilding The Imagination

One of my friends, the pianist Michael Jones, recently said in a conversation with a circle of friends dedicated to bringing Sidhe-ness into our lives, that we need to *"rewild the imagination"*.

This is so to the point of what is urgently needed and at hand right now. Imagination is our prison and our freedom. It depends on what we do with it. To put it paradoxically, we have tamed the imagination into unimaginable boredom! There is a tremendous task in liberating it from predictable framing and control. This requires audacity and hungry curiosity. If we consistently expect reality to be a certain way, we frame and select our perception and omit any real surprise.

To the Sidhe imagination is not something they have. Imagination is something they are. This is provocative to the role of consensus rationality in our present civilization. We consider imagination to be a private and isolated thing and often we share our peculiar images with others. Sometimes we create a shared field, but the field arises from what we think is an individual creation. The Sidhe can help us understand that this does not need to be the only reality. As the female Sidhe, Mariel, has shared with David Spangler:

"For you, imagination is a subjective experience. For us it is objective. It is a quality of fluidity and responsiveness within the life of the matter that forms the substance of our world. It is why our world is so directly responsive to our thoughts. In a way, you might say that we live in imagination. This is true for you, too, but it is not so obvious because of the solidity of your world. Thought crystallizes more densely in your version of the physical dimension. Imagination bifurcates into what is within you and what is outside you... For us, imagination refers to a primal quality of matter. Think of it as grace within matter, the protean power to respond to creative will. It is a fluidity of being... We do not possess imagination individually as much as we participate in the "ocean of imagination" that is part of the life of the world. This does not mean that we cannot form images or imagine new forms as you do, but we do so in collaboration with the flow of imagination within the world."

("Conversations with the Sidhe", p. 11-14)

This perception has tremendous implications. We can learn immensely from this if we tap more into the flow of wholeness. As AE says: *"We are what we imagine"* (*"The Candle of Vision"*, p. 24), and *"We have imagined ourselves into littleness, darkness, and ignorance, and we have to imagine ourselves back into light."* (AE in letter to Sean O'Faolain, Oct. 1933, Eglinton: Memoir of AE, p. 258.) A lack of wide perception and open imagination is spiritual oxygen-deprivation. We desperately need fresh air, and we also need this 'air' to come with grace, with gentleness, freed from arrogance or a stubborn, mental sense of superiority.

The greatest change factor in our lives regarding the climate crisis is if we can create a radical, inner climate change. This can start happening if we are willing to take excursions away from our mental boxes of predictability and sense the greater flow of wholeness. Instead of insisting only on our originality and individual independence, we can lean into the greater flow of life around us and listen to the needs of Gaia, the vast wholeness of the Earth. Today there are many, many small signs of this around the globe resulting in a kind of rudimentary 'Gaian thinking', imagining how the wellbeing of all life can be served, and not just the limited human part of the vast sphere of planetary life. We need a wave of inventions and a wave of support for these tiny seeds so they can grow and take solid shape.

When we begin to seriously take the needs of an octopus or an ant as a member of an equally respectful planetary co-species, we start moving in the right direction. When we ask the fields, what is the best for them, we take upon us the mantle of responsible citizenship. When we are willing to adapt and change to help other than our own species, we show signs of soul awakening. When we start tuning into the needs of Gaia and not just ourselves, we mature and start leaving our teenage phase of human life.

Deep listening to the life of Gaia, the living planet, is to take our home seriously. This is not a rigid discipline or a grave role. It should bring back into our lives a playfulness, curiosity, and a joyful artfulness. It is part of our inherent and mature innocence. We leave the dull predictiveness behind and move with the wind. We see what we never deeply perceived before, and we wonder why it took such a long time to start co-breathing and co-living with our planetary neighbors.

Regenerative Leadership

In a communication with David Spangler in April 2021, his Sidhe contact Mariel talked about the need to let "Sidhe-ness" be discovered in our collective and cultural institutions. She said:

"… in understanding the scale of this work, you must realize that work within and upon your institutions—the organs of collective energy flow—is an important part of this collaborative process and well within the arena of possible cooperation and co-creation between us. Invite us into your institutional and organizational lives as much and as joyously as you invite us into your environmental and artistic and cultural lives. We can help, but only when we are asked, for it is in the asking that you begin to loosen the grip of centuries of habit, fear, and selfishness that bind your organizations into the structures they present."

There are many uplifting signs in this discovery and the process to awaken to new roles within the planetary wholeness, no matter how unconscious the awareness of the Sidhe may be. One of these is the very nature of leadership. We need to discover a deep leadership to take on the core purpose of our being in the world. Leadership in a completely new sense will never be a matter of dominance and dictatorship but will be the adult function of our co-being with each other and other species. There is no need to mention the Sidhe in this process. Without verbal explanation, we can lean into the connectedness of our natural being, and gradually begin to form partnerships within the planetary whole. It is a matter of mentality and consciousness.

There are many such new impulses in the making today. One of them is called "Regenerative Leadership", developed by Giles Hutchins and Laura Storm. Both are well accomplished in the world of business and leadership and are recognized for coining the term Regenerative Leadership and developing it as a new blueprint for modern organizations. Their approach is deeply woven into the need for sustainability and co-creative evolution and aims toward building truly regenerative and life affirming organizations that revolve around living systems and learn from the wisdom of nature.

Just as humankind has learned and mastered multiple things from the scientific and technological revolutions, we now need to integrate knowledge with deep learnings from the wisdom of nature. This implies reclaiming our own inner nature with the connection to outer nature and restructuring our ways of living to be attuned to the deep logic and intelligence of life. In addition to being a new discovery, it is also a healing process. It weaves leadership with indigenous insights such as universal traits of shamanism and cyclical flow.

Regenerative Leadership recognizes what it calls 'the logic of life': That the life-affirming approach is an over-arching principle; that life is ever-changing and responsive; that we need to engage in relational and collaborative ways; that the presence of diversity and synergy is everywhere; that the rhythmical seasons of ebb and flow penetrate everything; that life depends on flows of energy and matter; and that we are all imbedded in an all-pervasive field of living systems. Just sensing the atmosphere of such an approach in all its humaneness is to begin hearing the notes of the Call of the Sidhe. The living systems field is the deep connectedness of the Gaian being and it is always, without exception, life-affirming to re-enter the great river of life and its constant renewal. It is a logic that is lyrical and a language that is a song.

The Call Onwards

We need to discover and heed the planetary impulses that are already here. Waiting for a better tomorrow is to postpone it into oblivion. The future is sprouting all around us in the here and now. What do we need to look for? I am sure these impulses will have the signs of livingness, of renewal and a letting go of rigid structures that strangle life. By its very nature this call will have a touch of effortlessness, an approach that is flowing like water or moving like the wind and makes life more playful and in a certain way, unpredictable. There may be a tingle of craziness of that which is not conformed and compromised but is leaning into "why not?" and "never thought before". The new seeds of tomorrow will have the freshness of the real and the practical in ways that invite a greater embodiment and not only theoretical speculations. A plasticity and lightness will be enlivened and no matter how heavy the implications may be, there will emerge pathways to solutions through undogmatic and unconventional ways. Behind everything there will be a palpable connectedness with the greater whole and when listening to the hum of life, there will be an invitation for dancing and musicality which is the signature of the Sidhe.

So, are you and I present in this time now and focused on these new seeds? There is a song in the world right now. It is the Call of the Sidhe, but at the same time it is the Call of our Sidhe-ness in all our Humaneness. This song reaches back into the ancient past and points forward into the never dared future - it is the "ancient future", or the deep present. In this intense aliveness, brimming with ecstatic renewal, you and I are called to open our glimmering lips:

"To breathe some wondrous story."
— (AE, A Call of the Sidhe)

Selected literature

The Sidhe

Jeremy Berg: *Faery Blood*, Lorian Press 2013.

Steve Blamires: *The Chronicles of the Sidhe*, Skylight Press 2012.

W. Y. Evans-Wentz: *The Fairy-Faith in Celtic Countries*, Dover Publications 2002.

Brian Froud & John Matthews: *How to see Faeries*, ABRAMS 2011.

Søren Hauge: *The Wild Alliance,* Lorian Press 2015.

Søren Hauge: *Finding Your Elvenheart,* Findhorn Press 2020.

Diarmuid Mac Manus: *Irish Earth Folk*, The Devin-Adair Company 1959.

John Matthews: *The Sidhe – Wisdom from the Celtic Underworld,* Lorian Press 2007.

David Spangler, art by Jeremy Berg: *Card Deck of the Sidhe*, Lorian Press 2011.

David Spangler: *A Midsummer's Journey with the Sidhe*, Lorian Press 2011.

David Spangler: *Partnering with Earth – The Incarnation of a Soul*, Lorian Press 2013.

David Spangler: *Conversations with the Sidhe*, Lorian Press 2014.

David Spangler: *Engaging with the Sidhe – Conversations Continued*, Lorian Press 2017.

William Butler Yeats

W. B. Yeats: *The Works of W. B. Yeats*, Wordsworth Poetry Library, Wordsworth Editions Ltd. 1994.

W. B. Yeats: *Collected Poems*, Macmillan Collector's Library 2010.

W. B. Yeats: *The Book of Fairy and Folk Tales* – Compiled by W. B. Yeats, Bounty Books, reprinted 2016.

AE (George William Russell)

AE: *Collected poems* 1913, https://www.bartleby.com/people/RusslG.html

AE: *Selected Poems*, The Swan River Press, Dublin 2017.

AE (George William Russell): *The Candle of Vision*, Quest Books 1974.

AE (G. W. Russell): *The Descent of the Gods,* part 3, ed. By Raghaven & Nandini Iyer, Colin Smythe 1988.

Marcus Beale: *Paintings by George W. Russell (AE)*, Printed by Nicholson & Bass Ltd. 2006

John Eglinton: *A Memoir of AE, George William Russell,* Coracle Press, 2007.

Henry Summerfield: *That Myriad-Minded Man, a Biography of George William Russell,* Colin Smythe 1975.

Other Selected Sources

Giles Hutchins & Laura Storm: *Regenerative Leadership, the DNA of Life-Affirming 21st century Organizations*, Wordzworth 2019.

Michael Jones: *Creating an Imaginative Life*, Pianoscapes 2006.

Jay Griffiths: *WILD – An Elemental Journey*, Penguin Books 2008.

Websites

Lorian Association: www.lorian.org
David Spangler: www.davidspangler.com
Jeremy Berg: www.lorianpress.com
Søren Hauge: www.wildheart.land

About The Publisher

Lorian Press LLC is a private, for profit business which publishes works approved by the Lorian Association.

Current titles by David Spangler and others can be found on the Lorian website www.lorian.org and at www.lorianpress. com.

The Lorian Association is a not-for-profit educational organization. Its work is to help people bring the joy, healing, and blessing of their personal spirituality into their everyday lives. This spirituality unfolds out of their unique lives and relationships to Spirit, by whatever name or in whatever form that Spirit is recognized. For more information, go to www. lorian.org.

www.ingramcontent.com/pod-product-compliance
Lightning Source LLC
Chambersburg PA
CBHW051213090426
42742CB00021B/3436